Year 2

Storybook Maths

Elaine Bennett
and Jenny Critcher

Introduction

Why Storybook Maths?

As dedicated infant practitioners, we have used stories daily in our teaching across the age range from the Early Years to the end of Key Stage 1. We have seen young children demonstrate delight and interest as they become familiar with, and grow to love, stories and the characters in them. This was the inspiration behind our idea to use stories as a vehicle for teaching maths and other areas of the curriculum.

When trying to find resources to support this approach, the only books we could find offered a limited number of activities that did not span the whole maths curriculum or age range. In some books, maths was not even mentioned, while links to subjects such as literacy and history were plentiful. This inspired us to develop resources to use within our school.

Our belief is that children learn and develop their mathematical knowledge and skills most successfully when provided with practical, engaging, real-life contexts. These can make maths something they feel involved in and excited about. Teaching maths through stories provides a natural way to embed 'using and applying', giving children a wealth of opportunities to consolidate and apply their understanding. Less confident children find stories a non-threatening way into learning. In addition, traditional tales can provide reassurance to children who are already familiar with the context.

We now know the importance of developing children's speaking and listening skills as part of their maths learning. Stories provide an ideal vehicle for talk as well as developing confidence with mathematical vocabulary.

Benefiting our VIPs!

The main aim of all practitioners is to nurture and inspire the 30 or so little VIPs in our classrooms. We aim to make our children feel positive about maths and believe that it is real and relevant to them. With storybooks as a focus, children work with a purpose and are motivated to learn. How much more exciting is it to weigh the contents of Red Riding Hood's baskets than classroom scissors and pencils!

Because children can relate to stories at their own level, stories provide teachers with opportunities for differentiation. Children also feel empowered to make decisions about their own learning. If maths is allowed to extend beyond a one-hour session, children have the time to explore and develop problem-solving strategies and approaches.

The bigger picture

There is nothing better than joining in children's excitement about what they are learning. Over the past few years, we have shared many special moments with each other and support staff when children have become immersed in the imaginative world of stories and totally enthralled with their learning in maths. The excitement of going to a 'school fair' (in the classroom), where children spend their money on stalls such as 'Hook a duck', 'Toy sale' and 'Coconut shy', resulted in children telling their parents in loud voices "I haven't done any work; we've played all day!" when, in fact, we knew they had been using and applying their mathematical understanding and taking some real steps in learning.

Maths through stories has become a whole-school approach, with each year group using stories that link to current topics while ensuring coverage of the curriculum.

Making links with parents is important if children are to reach their full potential. If you let parents know which stories are going to be used in maths teaching, they can share these stories at home with their children, either reading from books or retelling familiar tales. Parents are often not sure of how to support maths at home. Reading and telling these stories at home will remind children of the exciting activities that they have done that day or week. As children talk about what they have been doing at school, they help their parents see how to support their child's maths learning.

Getting started

• The activities in this book are not intended to provide a scheme of work to be followed; nor are they an exhaustive list. They offer an enjoyable and exciting collection of ideas to be shared, added to and dipped into with colleagues.

• It has taken time for stories to become embedded into the maths curriculum in our school. A good way for you to start would be to choose one story from the book, select one or more activities you like the sound of and dip your toe in the water.

• A bolder alternative is to start with a 'storybook maths week', where each class or year group focuses on one book for a week, working across the curriculum, but with a maths focus. We have done this in our school, and it was a great success: staff, children, parents and governors all had fun!

• In maths, there will always be skills that you need to teach directly. Once you have introduced them, children can develop their confidence in the skills, consolidating and applying them through work on stories.

• Above all ... enjoy!

How to use this book

This book has seven sections, all following the same format: three relate to modern stories and four to traditional ones. Each section offers ideas for activities on all the seven strands of maths, but focuses in particular on one of these strands:

• Using and applying mathematics

• Counting and understanding number

• Knowing and using number facts

• Calculating

• Understanding shape

• Measuring

• Handling data

Each story suggests links with possible topics, which you may find useful in your planning. For example, if you are going to do some work on food and healthy eating as well as safety issues, *Hansel and Gretel* is a good story to use and, mathematically, would give you opportunities to work on using and applying maths. If you have work planned on different cultures and how they celebrate certain events, then consider introducing *Cinderella* and do some work on counting and understanding number.

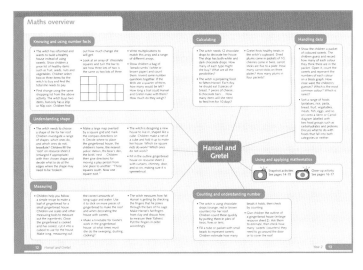

The maths overview outlines ideas for activities on six strands of maths and suggestions for taking some of the maths outdoors.

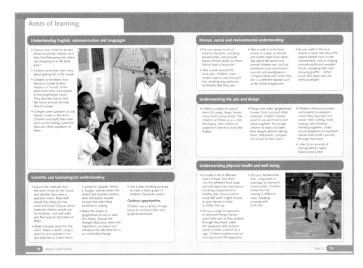

This section outlines opportunities for learning in other areas of the curriculum. There are brief suggestions for activities in:

• Understanding English, communication and languages

• Scientific and technological understanding

• Human, social and environmental understanding

• Understanding the arts and design

• Understanding physical health and well-being

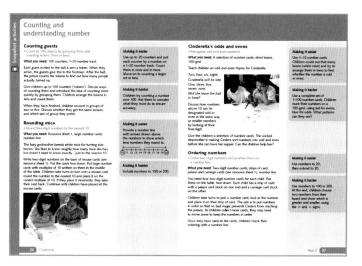

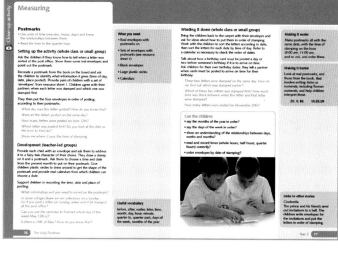

The four snapshot activities concentrate on one strand of maths. They are more detailed than those on the previous two pages, and each one is matched to a particular learning objective.

The close-up activity offers a detailed lesson plan, focussing on the same strands of maths as the snapshot activities. There are also ideas for differentiating the activity for children working at different levels.

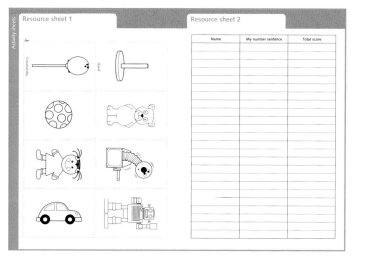

Each chapter contains two resource sheets. These are not worksheets, but contain templates for cards and props that we have found ourselves making numerous times over the years, and which we refer to in the activities earlier in the chapter.

You can adapt the sheets in various ways by enlarging, reducing or amending as necessary.

How to use this book

The close-up activity focuses on the same strand of maths as the snapshot activities.

Resources you need to carry out the activity

Links to the mathematics framework. The activity may cover several aspects of maths, but the main objective addressed is given here.

You can do the activity with the whole class or introduce it to a group at a time. We illustrate one way you can start off the activity, but you can adapt it as you see fit. We suggest a few things for you to say during this initial phase, to draw out children's explanations and to help them clarify their thinking.

As with the setting-up section, here you find suggestions about how to develop and wind down the session as well as what to say when discussing the activity with children to draw them out mathematically.

Close-up activity

Knowing and using number facts

Beanstalk race

- Use knowledge of number facts and operations to check answers to calculations
- Derive and recall all addition and subtraction facts for each number to at least 10, all pairs with totals to 20 and all pairs of multiples of 10 with totals to 100

Setting up the activity (whole class or small group)

Work with the children on a copy of the beanstalk. Roll the 1–6 dice to find the starting number and write this on the bottom leaf. Next, roll both dice, agree the operation they show (such as −3 or +6) and ask the children to carry out that operation on the starting number. Record the answer on the second leaf. Continue like this until you reach the top, each time operating on the number from the previous leaf. Put the final total on the cloud.

Discuss any issues that come up and remind children that addition can be done in any order, but subtraction cannot. Agree that if they cannot carry out an operation such as 2 − 6, they roll the dice again.

Can you explain why we can't do 5 − 6?

Do you think that when we get to the top, we will have got above 15? Why do you think that?

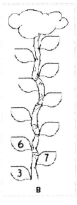

B

Development (teacher-led groups)

Children work in pairs to complete a beanstalk in the same way.

If you were at the top of the beanstalk and wanted to get back to the bottom, how could you do it?

What could you try next?

Can you tell me what you have been doing today?

If your friend was stuck, what could you say to help them?

Winding it down (whole class or small group)

Bring children back to the carpet and share some examples of work. Look at one beanstalk and challenge children to work out, by looking at the numbers on the leaves, which operations were carried out each time.

40 *Jack and the Beanstalk*

What you need

- Copies of Beanstalk B from resource sheet 1 (one cop for each pair of children)
- 1–6 dice
- Dice showing ' + + + + −
- Pencils
- Number lines (optional)
- 1–10 dice (optional)

Useful vocabulary

calculate, sign, operation, symbol, problem, solution, calculation, inverse, answer method, add, subtract, sum total, plus, minus, take awa equals, count on, count ba

As children work, observe what they do and say in order to make on-the-spot assessments. The more you can note down in class, the more food for thought afterwards as you reflect on the children's work and their achievements.

...cord these operations.

...xt, ask children to start at the top of the beanstalk and ...rk out the operations needed to get back to the bottom. ...cord these operations.

Look at these two beanstalks: can you see any similarities ...or differences?

5 is on this leaf, and 10 is on this one. How did Priti get ...from 5 to 10?

Can the children
* work out addition and subtraction problems quickly and confidently? Do they work mentally or practically?
* look at the numbers on two next-door leaves and work out which operation was used to get from one to the other?
* explain to a partner what they have done?
* show an understanding of addition and subtraction and their relationship?
* record number sentences correctly?

Making it easier

Support children as they use number lines to work out the problems.

Making it harder

Children choose a number to put at the bottom of their beanstalk and another one to put in the cloud. They work out how to get from the bottom to the top.

Instead of a 1–6 dice, use a 1–10 dice; include '×' on the operations dice.

Adapt the activity to children working at different levels by making it easier or harder.

Links to other stories

Hansel and Gretel
Children leave pebbles to mark their trail through the forest, but can only find their way back home if they put the correct numbers on each pebble.

Other possible story contexts for this activity to achieve the same mathematical purpose

Maths vocabulary that you might want to use in talking with children about their work

Hansel and Gretel

This well-known traditional tale was first collected and recorded by the Brothers Grimm in 19th-century Germany. It is a story about two children who are abandoned in a forest by their father and stepmother. Hansel has the idea of leaving a trail of breadcrumbs to find the way back home, but the hungry birds eat the crumbs, and the children are lost.

When they come across a gingerbread house, all their worries seem to be over. Unfortunately, the tasty house belongs to a witch who locks Gretel in the house and fattens Hansel for the pot. Gretel succeeds in saving herself and her brother, and they escape a dismal fate ...

The story is rich in possibilities for all sorts of work and is worth exploring in its own right. You can also introduce it as part of work on food and healthy eating or general health and safety issues.

Maths overview

Knowing and using number facts

- The witch has reformed and wants to build a healthy house instead of using sweets. Show children a price list of healthy items such as fruit, seeds, nuts and vegetables. Children select two or three items for the witch to buy and find the total she needs to pay.

- Find change using the same shopping list from the above activity. The witch buys two items, but only has a 20p or 50p coin. Children find out how much change she will get.

- Look at an array of chocolate squares and turn the bar to see how three lots of two is the same as two lots of three.

Write multiplications to match this array and a range of different arrays.

- Show children a bag of 'breadcrumbs' (white or brown paper) and count them. Invent some number questions together. If the birds ate a quarter of them, how many would be left? How long a trail could Hansel and Gretel make with them?

Understanding shape

- The witch needs to choose a shape of tile for her roof. Children investigate a range of shapes: which ones do, and which ones do not, tessellate? Children fill the 'roof' on resource sheet 2 (enlarged if appropriate) with their chosen shape and decide what to do at the edges where the shape may need to be 'broken'.

- Make a large map overlaid by a square grid and mark the compass directions on it. Decide where to place the gingerbread house, the children's home, the nearest police station, the bear's den, the birds' nest … Children then give directions for moving a play person from one place to another: "Three squares south. Now one square east."

- The witch is designing a new house to live in, shaped like a cube. Children make a net of a cube and fold it up to make her house. Which six-square nets do work? Which ones do not work?

- Fill in the outline gingerbread house on resource sheet 2 with curtains, chimney, door, and so on, making sure it is symmetrical.

Measuring

- Children help you follow a simple recipe to make a loaf of gingerbread for a small gingerbread house. Children use scales and other measuring tools to measure out the ingredients. Once the gingerbread is cooked and has cooled, cut it into a cuboid to use for the house. Make icing, measuring out the correct amounts of icing sugar and water. Use it to stick on more pieces of gingerbread to make the roof and when decorating the house with sweets.

- Make a timetable for Gretel's work in the gingerbread house: at what times must she do the sweeping, dusting, cooking?

- The witch measures how fat Hansel is getting by checking the fingers that he pokes through the bars of his cage. Make Hansel's fat fingers from clay and discuss how to measure their 'fatness'. Put the fingers in order accordingly.

Calculating

- The witch needs 12 chocolate drops to decorate her house. The shop has both white and dark chocolate drops. How many of each type might she buy? What are all the possibilities?

- The witch is preparing food to fatten Hansel. Each day, he should eat 3 pieces of bread, 7 pieces of cheese, 6 chocolate bars … How many items will she need to feed him for 10 days?

- Gretel finds healthy treats in the witch's cupboard. Dried plums come in packets of 10, cherries come in twos, carrot sticks are five to a plate. How many carrot sticks on three plates? How many plums in four packets?

Handling data

- Show the children a packet of coloured sweets. The children guess and record how many of each colour they think there are in the packet. Open it, count the sweets and represent the numbers of each colour on a block graph. How close were the children's guesses? Which is the most common colour? Which is rarest?

- Sort a range of foods (potatoes, rice, pasta, bread, fruit, vegetables, meats, fish, eggs, and so on) onto a Venn or Carroll diagram labelled with two food groups such as carbohydrates and proteins. Discuss what to do with foods that fall into both categories or neither.

Hansel and Gretel

Using and applying mathematics

 Snapshot activities
See pages 14-15

 Close-up activity
See pages 16-17

Counting and understanding number

- The witch is using chocolate drops (orange, red or brown counters) for her roof. Children count these quickly by putting them in piles of twos, fives or tens.

- Fill a tube or packet with small beads to represent sweets. Children estimate how many beads it holds, then check by counting.

- Give children the outline of a gingerbread house (enlarge resource sheet 2). Ask them to estimate, then check how many 'sweets' (counters) they need to go around the door or to cover the roof.

Using and applying mathematics

Sponge roof tiles

- Present solutions to puzzles and problems in an organised way
- Explain decisions, methods and results in pictorial, spoken or written form, using mathematical language

What you need: Brown and white paper squares (tiles)

The witch is going to make the roof of her house using sponge tiles. Each row is six tiles long and consists of three chocolate and three vanilla tiles.

Children work out a sequence of sponge tiles using the two flavours: for example V V V C C C or V C V C V C.

The witch wants each row of tiles to be different. What different arrangements of the six tiles can the children make? Ask them to think about how to record their work: using coloured pencil dots, letters for the flavours, coloured counters. Remind them to check that none of their arrangements is the same.

Making it easier

Work with four tiles in a row: two chocolate and two vanilla.

Making it harder

Discuss how to work and record systematically. Ask children how they might extend the problem.

Witch's biscuits

- Follow a line of enquiry
- Answer questions by selecting, organising and presenting information in lists, tables and simple diagrams

What you need: Ready-prepared table or tally chart

The witch plans to tile her roof with biscuits. She wants to make sure that her house appeals to as many children in the class as possible.

What information does she need to collect in order to find out the class's favourite biscuits? Should she use just one kind of biscuit on the roof, or two, or several?

Children discuss her problem, then collect the relevant information and agree how to present it to her.

Making it easier

Give children a ready-prepared table or tally chart to collect and present their information.

Making it harder

Children prepare a report for the witch, explaining what they think she should do and giving their reasons.

Gingerbread trays

• Solve problems involving addition and multiplication in the context of numbers

What you need: Squared paper

The witch is building her gingerbread house and buys gingerbread in large trays. Each tray holds 10 pieces of gingerbread. If she needs to buy 44 pieces of gingerbread, how many trays does she need to buy? The children explain how they work out the answer to the problem.

What if she needed 84 pieces of gingerbread?

Making it easier

Help children model the problem with arrays of 10 squares (squared paper) to represent trays of gingerbread.

Making it harder

Some trays hold 10 pieces of gingerbread, and some hold 12. The witch needs 84 pieces. What is a sensible combination of trays to buy?

Symmetrical vegetables

• Describe patterns and relationships involving shapes, make predictions and test these with examples

What you need: Potatoes or large carrots, paints; counters, assymetrical shapes

Children use vegetable prints to make a symmetrical design for the witch's front door. Start with one or two shapes and one or two colours. As children become more confident, encourage them to try more complex designs. Use mirrors to check for symmetry.

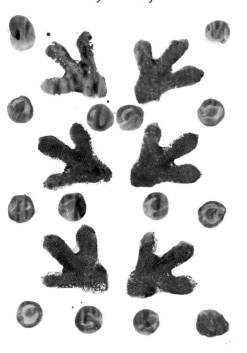

Making it easier

Children use round or square counters instead of, or as a preliminary, to printing.

Making it harder

Give children some asymmetrical shapes with which to print and ask them to explore whether it is possible to use these to make a symmetrical design.

Using and applying mathematics

Visiting the cake shop

- Solve problems involving addition, subtraction, multiplication or division in the context of pounds and pence
- Identify and record the information or calculation needed to solve a puzzle or problem; carry out the steps or calculations and check the solution in the context of the problem

Setting up the activity (whole class or small group)

With the children's help, set up a role-play area as a cake shop and display cakes in. Provide coins in a till.

Involve the children in pricing objects (make sure they include one- and two-digit numbers in the prices to ensure adequate differentiation) and encourage them to write a price list.

How shall we sort out the coins?

Have we got enough 5p coins?

What shall we charge for cream-filled cakes? And for a piece of shortbread?

Development (teacher-led groups)

The witch is visiting the cake shop to buy material for a new house, but needs the children's help, as she is not very good at numbers and money. Each child chooses two cakes to buy for her from the shop.

Before buying the cakes, children work out the total they must pay. Encourage them to use jottings or equipment such as a number line or coins to find the total.

Take on the role of shopkeeper and sell them the cakes. Children record an addition sentence as a way of explaining to the witch how they spent her money.

7p
Gingerbread

5p
Cherry cake

7p + 5p = 12p

Extend this to buying three cakes. Prompt children to think about the quickest way to add three prices together, using knowledge of number bonds, starting from the largest number, adding near doubles ...

What you need

- Role-play equipment for the cake shop: playdough cakes and buns or pictures (use resource sheet 1 and add your own)
- Price tags, till, real coins
- 0–30 number line

Useful vocabulary

money, coin, penny, pence, pound, price, pay, change, cost, how much?, total, add, equals, plus, calculate, method

Give children an amount of money such as 50p or 35p in coins. Ask them to find out what is the greatest number of cakes they can buy and whether they will get any change. Again, encourage children to use informal jottings to support their working out.

What calculation could you do to find the total?

What could you use to help you find the answer?

Which calculation could you do in your head? How do you do that?

What is the smallest number of coins you could use to pay 12p?

How could you record your working out?

Winding it down (whole class or small group)

All groups have completed the activity.
Give each group a character or food name, then take one of each 'character' or 'food item' to make a new group. Continue until every child is in a new group. Each child takes turns in their new group to talk about the calculations and strategies they have been using in their activities.

Only one group has completed the activity.
Ask each child to discuss with a partner which parts of the activity they found the hardest, which the easiest, and what they used to help them.

Can you explain how you solved the problem?

What could you try if we did this again?

Can the children

- find totals using appropriate mental strategies?

- talk about the strategies or methods they have used, and what they could try next time?

- use a number line or other equipment to help them with their calculations?

- use informal jottings to support their working out?

- choose and record the correct calculation?

- carry out the steps of the calculation to find the answer?

Making it easier

Children buy one item at the cake shop and record which coins they could use to pay with. Extend to buying two items costing under 10p.

Making it harder

Include some cakes at higher prices.

Ask children to do some multiplications and divisions: how much would 5 Battenburg cakes cost? How many slices of cherry cake can they buy for £1? Help children record using the '×' and '÷' signs.

Links to other stories

Dogger
Set up a shop for Dave to visit to buy some new toys.

The Jolly Postman
Set up a post office with cards, stamps and envelopes on sale.

Growing Good
Set up a gardening shop with plants and seeds on sale.

Areas of learning

Understanding English, communication and languages

- Discuss how it feels to be lost. What should the children do if they find themselves lost when out shopping or in the local area?

- Children write their own story about getting lost in the woods.

- Children write letters from Hansel or Gretel to their relations or friends, at the point when they are trapped in the gingerbread house. They describe how to find the house and ask for help how to escape.

- Compile some questions to ask Hansel, Gretel or the witch. Children and adults then take turns at hot-seating, while the class asks these questions of them.

Scientific and technological understanding

- Discuss the materials that the witch chose for her house, and whether they were a practical choice. How well would they keep out rain, wind and snow? Discuss which materials children would use for windows, roof and walls and find ways to test some of them.

- Make a burglar alarm for the witch. Make a switch using a piece of card covered in foil and attached to a wire which is joined to a buzzer. When a 'burglar' presses down the switch and touches another wire, the buzzer sounds to warn the witch that someone is coming.

- Make flat sheets of gingerbread to use as walls of a house. Discuss the changes that occur when the ingredients are baked and introduce the idea that this is an irreversible change.

- Use a data-handling package to make a block graph of children's favourite sweets.

Outdoor opportunities

Children use a variety of large boxes to construct their own gingerbread house.

Human, social and environmental understanding

- Put out various kinds of food for the birds, including breadcrumbs, and provide bowls of fresh water for them. Which food is favourite?

- Take a walk around the local area. Children make simple maps in case they got lost, marking any particular landmarks that they pass.

- Take a walk in some local woods or a park, as Hansel and Gretel might have done. Talk about the plants and animals children see, such as wildflowers and mushrooms, squirrels and woodpigeons ... Compare these with what they see in a different habitat such as the school playground.

- As you walk in the local woods or park, talk about the impact people have on the environment, such as making concrete paths and wooden fences, dropping litter and spraying graffiti ... What would this place look like without people?

Understanding the arts and design

- Collect a variety of natural items (fir cones, twigs, leaves, moss) from a local wood. The children set these up as a still-life display, then choose an angle from which to draw the display.

- Design and make 'gingerbread houses' from card and other materials. Children choose what to use and how to join pieces together. Encourage children to draw and label their designs before making them. Afterwards, compare the houses to their plans.

- Children choose percussion instruments to represent noises they may hear in a wood: trees rustling, birds singing, owls hooting ... Working together, create sound sequences to represent Hansel and Gretel's journey through the wood.

- Listen to an excerpt of Humperdinck's opera *Hansel and Gretel*.

Understanding physical health and well-being

- Compile a list of different kinds of food. Sort them into the different food types and talk about the importance of eating a balanced and healthy diet. Discuss which foods the witch might choose to give Hansel in order to fatten him up.

- Set up a range of apparatus to represent things Hansel and Gretel saw as they walked through the wood. Label the apparatus with pictures (posts as trees, a bench as a log). Children explore ways of moving around the apparatus.

- Set up a 'breadcrumb trail', using spots or beanbags to represent breadcrumbs. Children follow the trail, moving in different ways: hopping, jumping with both feet ...

Resource sheet 1

Battenburg

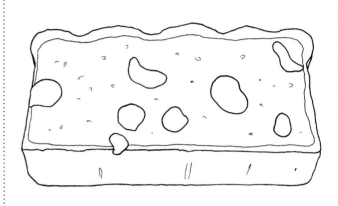

Cherry cake

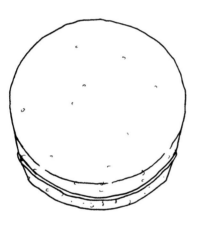

Cream-filled cake

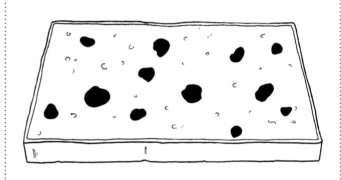

Fruitcake

Gingerbread

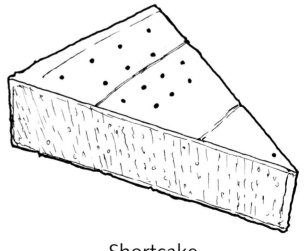

Shortcake

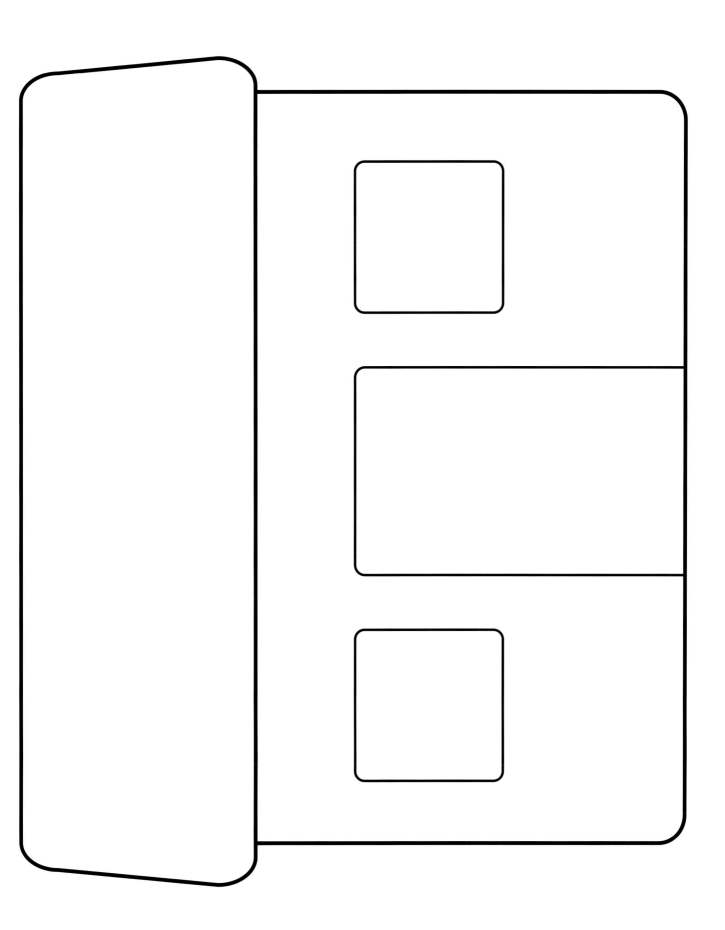

Cinderella

A much-loved story, its earliest version was recorded in China in the middle of the 9th century, and the heroine's helper was a magical fish!

Cinderella is deemed worthy only of sweeping the cinders from the fire and waiting on her stepmother and sisters as they prepare for the ball that she is not allowed to attend. But after the family has gone to the ball, Cinderella's fairy godmother arrives to transform her into a princess. There is only one condition: that she leaves the ball by midnight.

Once Cinderella is dancing with the prince, she forgets about this condition until she hears the clock begining to chime 12. As she dashes off, she leaves behind one glass slipper. This slipper gives the prince the chance of finding her again, and the story has a happy fairy-tale ending …

Use this story as part of work on parties and celebrations (feasts, weddings, naming ceremonies, festivals) or simply because it is a glorious tale in its own right.

Maths overview

Using and applying mathematics

- The fairy godmother has given Cinderella a tiara, a necklace and a bracelet for the ball. What combinations of accessories could Cinderella wear? Children record the possibilities and make sure they have got them all. What would happen if she had both a red and green tiara to choose from?

- The prince has a gold watch, a signet ring and a waistcoat to wear at the ball. What combinations of items could the prince wear? What if he also had a diamond tie pin? How many combinations would there be then?

- The fairy godmother buys a pumpkin to make the carriage for the ball. It costs 35p. She only has silver coins. What different combinations of coins could she use to pay for it? What if it cost 50p?

- The older ugly sister's shoe size is 12. To find Cinderella's shoe size, halve that number and subtract 1. What size are her shoes? Children make up more problems like this.

- At Cinderella and Prince Charming's wedding, the tables each seat 5 guests. Children decide how many tables they need for a given number of guests such as 32. Suppose the tables each sat 10 people? Suppose there were two sorts of table, some for 5 and some for 10 people? Children devise and record a seating plan.

Knowing and using number facts

- The fairy godmother's magic wand can double or halve things. Show pictures of things: mice, pumpkins, glass slippers (see resource sheet 1). Children work out how many of each item there will be after the spell.

- Use resource sheet 1 to make picture cards with numbers on them from 0 to 12 (or 15 or 20). Place them on the table, face down. Children pick two cards and look at the numbers; if their total is 12 (or 15 or 20) they keep the cards; if not, they put them back. The person who collects most cards is the winner.

Measuring

- Use clock faces to show various times: for example, 1:00, 8:30, 12:00. Ask the children to discuss what the prince or Cinderella might have been doing at these times. Tell the story again, adding the time of each event. Children show the time of each event on their own clock faces.

- Make a simple cake for Cinderella's wedding. Children choose suitable units and instruments and work with them to weigh the ingredients, using scales.

- Produce a selection of wrapped 'presents' for Cinderella's wedding. Children investigate the statement 'Are bigger presents always heavier?'.

- Provide some pretty shoes and Cinderella's foot measurements in centimetres. Which shoes would fit her best?

Calculating

- Write complete number sentences in a large script. Cover one of the numbers or signs with a glass slipper card (see resource sheet 1). The children work out what the glass slipper is hiding.

- Take on the role of fairy godmother, who uses a calculator to help her do calculations. Children choose a number to give to the fairy godmother, who performs an operation on it, such as ×5, in secret, then announces the answer. After a few turns with the same operation, the children say what operation she was doing.

Handling data

- Blow up some party balloons and weigh them down with clothes pegs. Discuss ways to sort them. Use a large Venn or Carroll diagram made on the floor with masking tape.

- Find out the most common shoe size in the class. Discuss with the children how to collect the information and present it. Consider using an ICT package for recording and presenting the data.

Cinderella

Counting and understanding number

 Snapshot activities
See pages 26-27

 Close-up activity
See pages 28-29

Understanding shape

- Transform a floor robot into Cinderella's coach and set up a route for it to travel along the floor (use boxes as buildings and masking tape to show the roads). Program the robot to travel between her home and the palace.

- Make a 'Pass the parcel' packet to use at the wedding party. How many layers are used? How much heavier is the final parcel than the gift inside? How much bigger?

- Cinderella doesn't have a coach to go to the ball, and the fairy godmother's magic has run out. Children design and make a carriage using straws, junk boxes, card …

Counting and understanding number

Counting guests

• Count to 100 objects by grouping them and counting in tens, fives or twos

What you need: 100 counters; 1–20 number track

Each guest invited to the ball is sent a token. When they arrive, the guests give this to the footman. After the ball, the prince counts the tokens to find out how many people actually turned up.

Give children up to 100 counters ('tokens'). Discuss ways of counting them and introduce the idea of counting more quickly by grouping them. Children arrange the tokens in tens and count them.

When they have finished, children recount in groups of two or five. Discuss whether they get the same answer, and which size of group they prefer.

Rounding mice

• Round two-digit numbers to the nearest 10

What you need: Resource sheet 1, large number cards; number line

The fairy godmother breeds white mice for turning into horses. She likes to know roughly how many mice she has, but doesn't need to know exactly – just to the nearest 10.

Write two-digit numbers on the back of mouse cards (see resource sheet 1). Put the cards face down. Put large number cards with multiples of 10 written on them in the middle of the table. Children take turns to turn over a mouse card, round the number to the nearest 10 and place it on the correct multiple of 10. If they place it incorrectly, they take their card back. Continue until children have placed all the mouse cards.

Making it easier

Use up to 20 counters and put each counter by a number on a 1–20 number track. Count them in ones and in twos. Move on to counting a larger set in tens.

Making it harder

Children try counting a number over 100. Ask them to consider what they must do to ensure accuracy.

Making it easier

Provide a number line with arrows drawn above the numbers to show which tens numbers they round to.

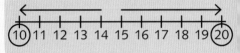

Making it harder

Include numbers to 150 or 200.

Cinderella's odds and evens

• Recognise odd and even numbers

What you need: A selection of number cards; dried beans, 100-grid

Teach children an odd and even rhyme for Cinderella:

Two, four, six, eight;
Cinderella will be late.
One, three, five,
seven, nine;
Will she leave the ball
in time?

Discuss how numbers above 10 can be designated odd or even in the same way as smaller numbers by looking at their final digit.

Give the children a selection of number cards. The wicked stepmother is making Cinders sort numbers into odd and even before she can have her supper. Can the children help her?

Ordering numbers

• Order two-digit numbers and position them on a number line

What you need: Two-digit number cards, strips of card, palace and carriage cards (see resource sheet 1), number line

You need four two-digit number cards for each child. Put these on the table, face down. Each child has a strip of card with a palace card stuck on one end and a carriage card stuck on the other.

Children take turns to pick a number card, look at the number and place it on their strip of card. The aim is to put numbers in order so that no bad magic prevents Cinders from reaching the palace. As children collect more cards, they may need to move some to keep the numbers in order.

Once they have used all the cards, children check their ordering with a number line.

Making it easier

Use 1–10 number cards. Children count out that many beans (white mice) and try to arrange them in twos to find whether the number is odd or even.

Making it harder

Use a complete set of 1–100 number cards. Children mark their numbers on a 100-grid, using red for evens, blue for odds. What patterns can they see?

Making it easier

Use numbers to 20, then extend to 30.

Making it harder

Use numbers to 100 or 200. At the end, children choose two numbers from their board and show which is greater and smaller, using the > and < signs.

Counting and understanding number

Mice, horses and pumpkins

- Explain what each digit in a two-digit number represents, including numbers where 0 is a place holder
- Partition two-digit numbers into multiples of 10 and 1

Setting up the activity (whole class or small group)

Show children the base 10-blocks (some tens and ones). Agree the number represented. Children show this with their number fans.

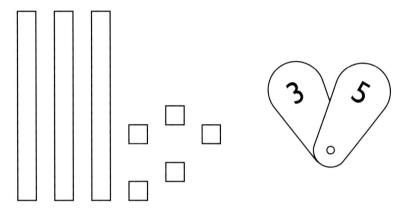

Play a version of 'What is my number?' where children show some tens and ones (or draw them on a wipeboard). The other children show the number with their fans, then say it.

Let's see if you can show the number that comes after 50 … The number just before 30.

How many tens are there in your number? And how many ones?

Development (teacher-led groups)

Explain that children are going to play a game based on tens and ones, using pumpkin coaches and white mice. Children take turns to roll the dice and put that many beans (white mice) on the mouse side of their board. They show the number of mice so far, in the space below, using digit cards.

When they have collected 10 white mice, they swap them for a coach (which needs 10 animals to pull it). They put back 10 beans and take a coach card to put on the coach side of the board.

What you need

- Base 10-blocks or linking cubes
- Number fans
- Wipeboards
- Resource sheet 1 (coach and horses cards; coloured if possible)
- 1–6 dice
- White beans
- 0–9 digit cards
- Resource sheet 2 (enlarged, for recording)
- Picture of a stable (optional)
- 1–20 dice or 10–20 spinner (optional)

Useful vocabulary

partition, zero, ten, twenty … one hundred, count in ones, units, tens, value, worth, two-digit

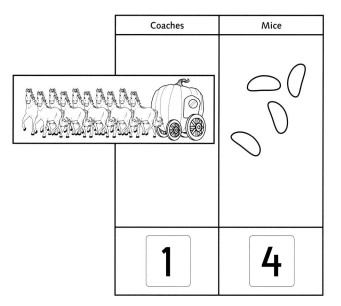

Coaches	Mice
1	**4**

Children continue for five to 10 minutes, then each child records the number of coaches they have accumulated, and how many spare mice they have.

How many mice do you have altogether now? One lot of 10 mice on that coach and another 4 makes …?

What two-digit number have you made? What does the number show?

How many more mice do you need to collect to get another coach?

Winding it up (whole class or small group)

Hold up, for example, 5 pumpkin coaches and 3 mice (beans). Children show the total number of mice with their number fans, and all say the number together.

Children then take turns to do the same thing.

Let's count the mice: 10, 20, 30 … 31, 32.

How do you know Harry has got 24 mice there?

Can the children

- show a given two-digit number with base 10-blocks (tens and ones)?
- explain what each digit in a two-digit number represents, using appropriate language?
- explain why they need to swap 10 mice for a coach card?
- record their work?

Making it easier

Stick 10 beans to a coach card to make it clear that the coach represents 10 mice. Make sure that if children have, for example, 12 beans on the mouse side, they don't put back all of their mice, but only 10 of them, when they swap for a coach card.

Making it harder

Introduce the idea of using three-digit numbers, partitioned into hundreds, tens and units. Use a picture of a grand stable (to hold 10 coaches) to represent 100 mice and use a 1–20 dice or a 10–20 spinner, aiming to reach at least 150 mice.

Links to other stories

Jack and the Beanstalk
Use beans as the units and bags of beans for tens.

Growing Good
Use pumpkin seeds (or nuts) as units and a pot of 10 seeds for tens.

Areas of learning

Understanding English, communication and languages

- Write invitations for the ball from the prince to the stepmother and her daughters.

- Write an account of the ball from the point of view of Cinderella or the prince.

- Write wedding invitations to fairy-tale characters from Cinderella and the prince.

- Write a wedding party menu.

Scientific and technological understanding

- Design a dress for Cinderella to wear to the ball. For safety reasons, Cinderella wants a fabric that you can see in the dark. Which colour would be the best to choose?

- Investigate what happens to the sound of the clock chime as Cinderella travels away from it. Does it get louder, quieter or stay the same?

- Write a newspaper report of the ball, with particular emphasis on the girl who left her shoe behind and the search that followed. Format the report using a word-processing program with columns.

- Wrap wedding presents, using as little paper as possible. Try using glue or tape and decide which sticks best.

Human, social and environmental understanding

- Look at the pictures in the storybook. Do they show a modern home and lifestyle or one from long ago? How can the children tell?

- Ask children to talk to family members about special balls or parties they have been to and to bring in photos, if possible. How were these events the same as or different from parties the children have experienced?

- Make a map of the route Cinderella took to get to the palace for the ball.

- Talk about places where you could have a ball or wedding in the local area. Locate the places on a local street map.

- Show pictures of local places where the prince's ball might be held. Discuss the features that give the places their character; debate which might be best for the ball, and why.

Understanding the arts and design

- In case the children lose their own shoe, ask them to complete an observational drawing of it to use in a 'Wanted' poster. Use a variety of drawing materials such as charcoal, pastels, pencil and paint and compare the results.

- Cinderella left the ball at midnight. Look at paintings such as 'Starry Night' by Van Gogh and discuss with the children how they depict night time. They then create their own interpretations of night time.

- Make envelopes for wedding invitations. Children take some envelopes apart to look at how they are made, then make their own. Try to make an envelope for an oddly sized or shaped invitation.

- Make a glass slipper for Cinderella, using a plastic drinks bottle and/or shimmery wrapping paper or fabric. Think about what shape it must be to fit a foot, and how to stick the pieces together.

- Play a variety of different-paced dances such as waltzes and tangos; children move in time to the music. Discuss how each piece made children feel, and what kind of movement felt appropriate.

Understanding physical health and well-being

- Talk about healthy and unhealthy food options, then plan a healthy menu for party food for the ball.

- Carve out the pumpkin to make the coach for Cinderella and use the insides for soup. Discuss how to prepare food hygienically and use tools safely.

- Children work with pairs or small groups to make up their own dance for the ball, practising sequences of movements and rehearsing in small groups. Pairs perform in turn during a class 'ball'.

Outdoor opportunities

Collect in ideas for party games and activities, then play some of them outdoors.

Make some healthy food and have an outdoors party.

Practise the different kinds of movements made by mice/horses as they pull the coach.

Resource sheet 1

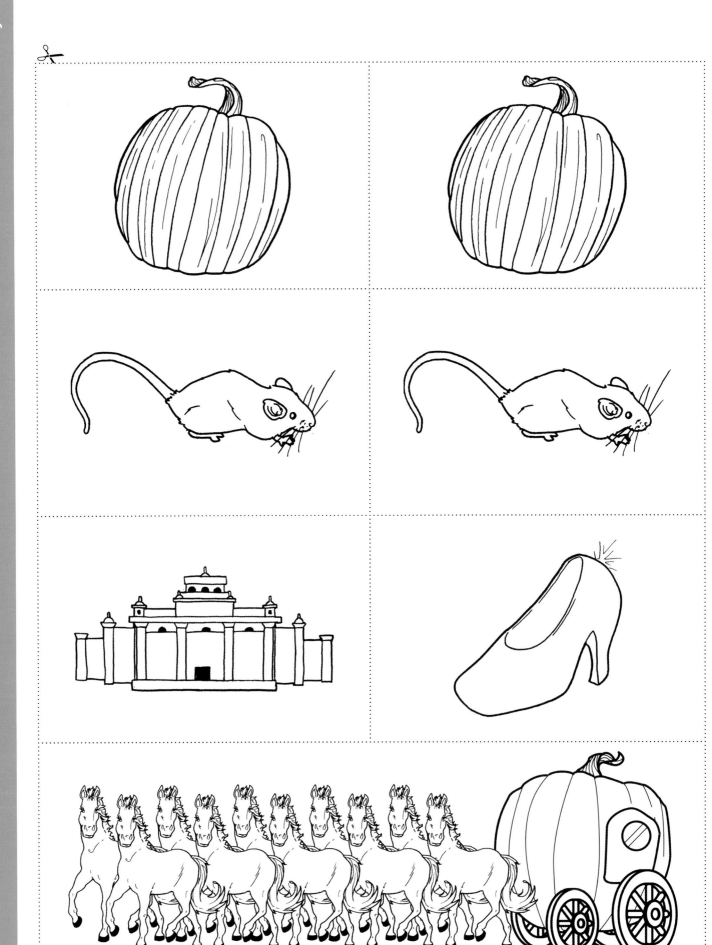

Coaches	Mice

Jack and the Beanstalk

The first recorded version of *Jack and the Beanstalk* appeared in the early 18th century in England. In the tale, the mother of a poor family sends her son Jack to market to sell the family cow. Much to the mother's dismay, Jack returns from market with some magic beans instead of money. When sown, the beans grow into a giant beanstalk which Jack climbs. In the giant's house at the top, Jack finds various magic things which he steals and brings home.

Use this story when you are working on growing plants, either for food or for other purposes, or weave it into work on magic lands or giants.

Maths overview

Using and applying mathematics

- Tell the children that the giant is twice as tall as they are and has footprints twice as long. They make the giant's footprints from paper.

- How many different ways can Jack climb the beanstalk? Use one of the beanstalks on resource sheet 1 to explore the various routes Jack could take: for example, left left, right right or left right, left right, and so on.

- Use beanstalk B with alternate leaves on resource sheet 1. Write a number such as 5 on the first leaf and a total such as 20 on the cloud at the top. Children 'climb' the beanstalk from 5 to 20 by writing a number to be added on each leaf. Move on to using subtraction as well as addition.

Counting and understanding number

- Use copies of beanstalk B on resource sheet 1 to make a twos, a fives and a tens beanstalk. Compare two of the beanstalks to find which numbers come up in both of them. If the beanstalks had more leaves and more numbers, would any numbers appear on all three beanstalks?

- Prepare a pile of green paper leaves. Children work in pairs. Each child rolls three dice, uses the digits to make the highest possible three-digit number and records this on a leaf. Their partner then does the same. The child whose leaf has the higher number wins a bean. Once each child has made five leaves, they arrange them in ascending order on a drawn beanstalk.

- Give children up to 100 beans for Jack to count. Ask them to help make it easier for Jack by grouping them into fives or tens.

Handling data

- Children explore which item the class would most like to own: gold coins, a hen or a harp. They use cards cut from resource sheet 2 as prompts, survey their classmates' opinions and record their findings.

- Cut out cards from resource sheet 2 and add some of your own. Explore imaginative ways of sorting them: living creatures, magic things, made from metal … Play a guessing game where one child sorts without revealing the criterion, which the other children try to guess.

Calculating

- Make a giant 2D beanstalk to stick to the wall. Stick cards cut from resource sheet 2 on different parts of the beanstalk. Estimate, then measure the height of each object from the ground.

- Write some measurements in centimetres on cards. Children pick a card and use a ruler to draw a beanstalk the given height. When children have done several, compare and discuss them. Which beanstalk is the tallest? The shortest? Are any two the same height?

- The giant gets thirsty and often gulps down a litre of juice in one go. Find containers that will hold this amount.

- The giant's wife drinks a cup of juice at a time. Help the children make a scale that measures cups, by drawing lines on an unmarked, see-through container with straight sides. How many cups are roughly equal to one litre?

Measuring

- Give children a number of beans (try 12, 13, 15, 16, 20, 21, 24, 25) to arrange in rectangular arrays on squared paper. Is there only one array that works for the chosen number?

- Jack tells his friends about the magic beans and they all want some. He has 20 spare beans to share between 5 friends. How many will each get? What is the next number of beans that would share fairly between them?

- Jack and his friends want to grow their beans. If 6 people each sow 4 beans, how many beans do they plant altogether?

Jack and the Beanstalk

Knowing and using number facts

 Snapshot activities
See pages 38-39

 Close-up activity
See pages 40-41

Understanding shape

- Children collect a range of leaves and investigate which ones are symmetrical and which ones are not. They record this on a chart.

- Children make a castle, using 3D solids, and take a photo of

it. They dismantle it, record how many of each shape were used and return them to their box. They ask a friend to use the same shapes, in the same quantities, to make their own castle. At the end, they compare this with the photo.

Knowing and using number facts

Multiplying beans

• Derive and recall multiplication facts for the 2, 5 and 10 times tables

What you need: 100-grid; dried beans

Jack has made packets containing five beans (or two or 10) and has taken them to market to sell. He sold three packets. How many beans was that altogether? Suppose he had sold six packets or 10 packets?

Work with the children to record the results for numbers of packets from 1 to 10 on a simple chart. Look at the numbers and shade the 'number sold altogether' values on a 100-grid. Talk with the children about the patterns they see.

5 beans in a packet	
Packets	Beans sold altogether
1	5
2	10
3	15
4	20
5	25

Making it easier

Work practically, putting beans into groups of five and counting how many there are altogether.

Making it harder

Children complete their own charts for 2, 3, 4 or 10 beans in a packet.

Planting beans

• Derive and recall all pairs with totals to 20

What you need: Two paper squares for each child

Jack and his friend have 20 beans to sow. They are going to sow some in Jack's garden and the rest in the friend's. Give children two 'gardens' (paper squares) to sow their beans in. How many different ways can they share the beans between the two gardens? Ask children to record the number pairs.

Making it easier

Work with a small group, sharing 5 or 10 beans between two gardens.

Making it harder

Expect children to record systematically.

Share 10 beans between three gardens.

Magic money bag

• Derive and recall doubles of all numbers to 20 and
  the corresponding halves

What you need: Resource sheet 2

Show children an enlarged picture of the money bag
from resource sheet 2. Some days, the money bag doubles
whatever you put in it, so if you put in 5 coins, they turn into
10 coins. Sometimes, it doesn't work so well and doesn't quite
manage the doubling: you put in 5 coins and it only turns
them into 7 or 8 coins.

Write up a day of the week. That day, the money bag is
functioning correctly. Pretend to put in a number of coins;
with fingers or number fans, the children show you the
number of coins you should get out.

Write up another day of the week. Today, you are not
sure whether the money bag is functioning correctly.
Pretend to put in a number of coins and tell the children
how many you have got out. They give you a thumbs
up if they think the money bag is working and a thumbs
down if they think it isn't.

Making it easier

Work with doubles to 5 + 5.

Making it harder

Work with a bag that halves
bad things, like rotten eggs and
poisonous beetles. Can children
halve odd numbers such as 5
and 11?

Double beanstalks

• Derive and recall doubles of all numbers to 20 and
  the corresponding halves

What you need: Resource sheet 1

Enlarge beanstalk A (see resource
sheet 1). Write numbers from 11 to
20 on the leaves on the left-hand
side, at random. Children write
the doubles of these numbers on
the leaves on the right.

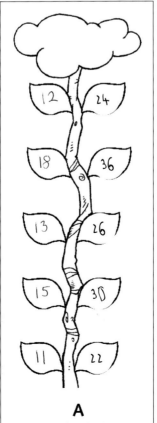

A

Making it easier

Stick to numbers up to 10.
Use counters, fingers or a
number line to help with
doubling numbers.

Making it harder

Work with higher numbers.

Children cover any number,
either on the left- or right-hand
side, with a counter. They
challenge a friend to say
what number is hidden
by the counter.

Knowing and using number facts

Beanstalk race

- Use knowledge of number facts and operations to check answers to calculations
- Derive and recall all addition and subtraction facts for each number to at least 10, all pairs with totals to 20 and all pairs of multiples of 10 with totals to 100

Setting up the activity (whole class or small group)

Work with the children on a copy of the beanstalk. Roll the 1–6 dice to find the starting number and write this on the bottom leaf. Next, roll both dice, agree the operation they show (such as -3 or $+6$) and ask the children to carry out that operation on the starting number. Record the answer on the second leaf. Continue like this until you reach the top, each time operating on the number from the previous leaf. Put the final total on the cloud.

Discuss any issues that come up and remind children that addition can be done in any order, but subtraction cannot. Agree that if they cannot carry out an operation such as $2-6$, they roll the dice again.

Can you explain why we can't do 5 − 6?

Do you think that when we get to the top, we will have got above 15? Why do you think that?

B

Development (teacher-led groups)

Children work in pairs to complete a beanstalk in the same way.

If you were at the top of the beanstalk and wanted to get back to the bottom, how could you do it?

What could you try next?

Can you tell me what you have been doing today?

If your friend was stuck, what could you say to help them?

Winding it down (whole class or small group)

Bring children back to the carpet and share some examples of work. Look at one beanstalk and challenge children to work out, by looking at the numbers on the leaves, which operations were carried out each time.

What you need

- Copies of Beanstalk B from resource sheet 1 (one copy for each pair of children)
- 1–6 dice
- Dice showing ' + + + + − − '
- Pencils
- Number lines (optional)
- 1–10 dice (optional)

Useful vocabulary

calculate, sign, operation, symbol, problem, solution, calculation, inverse, answer, method, add, subtract, sum, total, plus, minus, take away, equals, count on, count back

Record these operations.

Next, ask children to start at the top of the beanstalk and work out the operations needed to get back to the bottom. Record these operations.

Look at these two beanstalks: can you see any similarities or differences?

5 is on this leaf, and 10 is on this one. How did Priti get from 5 to 10?

Can the children

- work out addition and subtraction problems quickly and confidently? Do they work mentally or practically?

- look at the numbers on two next-door leaves and work out which operation was used to get from one to the other?

- explain to a partner what they have done?

- show an understanding of addition and subtraction and their relationship?

- record number sentences correctly?

Making it easier

Support children as they use number lines to work out the problems.

Making it harder

Children choose a number to put at the bottom of their beanstalk and another one to put in the cloud. They work out how to get from the bottom to the top.

Instead of a 1–6 dice, use a 1–10 dice; include '×' on the operations dice.

Links to other stories

Hansel and Gretel
Children leave pebbles to mark their trail through the forest, but can only find their way back home if they put the correct numbers on each pebble.

Areas of learning

Understanding English, communication and languages

- Discuss whether Jack was right to steal the giant's possessions. Is it ever right to steal? Write a letter from Jack to the giant and his wife, apologising for stealing their things.

- Retell the story from the perspective of the giant.

- Ask children to take on roles of the characters and explain their behaviour: "Mum, why were you so cross when Jack came back with the beans?"; "Jack, tell us why you stole some of the giant's possessions."

- Ask the children to describe the beanstalk and the giant. Use their ideas to make word banks of size words.

- Children grow their own beans and keep a diary with daily or weekly entries, detailing the growth of their plants.

- Make 'Missing' posters for the giant, offering rewards for the objects he has lost.

- The children imagine climbing their own beanstalk. Who and what do they find at the top?

Outdoor opportunities

Use large boxes and appropriate clothing to set up a role-play area for the giant's castle.

Scientific and technological understanding

- Look around the local area to identify plants growing in different environments. What kinds of plants grow in cool, damp areas? In sunny ones?

- Investigate conditions for plant growth by putting some spare plants in different places (in a cupboard, on a window sill, on the radiator). What happens to the plants, and why might that be?

Human, social and environmental understanding

- Is this story set in the present or the past? Look for clues.

- Look at pictures of castles and identify their features. Discuss the functions of these. Why did castles have arrow slits, drawbridges, moats?

- Talk about the cow Jack sold. Do families keep a single cow nowadays? Why is, or was, a cow useful? Where do we go for our dairy produce?

- Guess why the possessions were so special to the giant. What things are special to the children, and why? Talk about the sentimental value of objects versus their monetary value.

Understanding the arts and design

- Use plants as the subject of observational drawing, looking at the pattern and texture of the leaves, stem, roots …

- Work collaboratively to make a picture of a giant. Discuss what media to use.

- Use instruments to play the rhythm of 'Fe fi fo fum'. Play it quickly/slowly/loudly/quietly.

- Talk about the magic harp and look at pictures of harps. Look at a range of instruments and sort them into different families: stringed, wind, percussion …

- Make beanstalks from rolled newspaper stuck together with sticky tape. Which one is the tallest?

- Using a paint package, children make pictures of beanstalks and the magic land which is at the top.

Understanding physical health and well-being

- Use apparatus such as benches, mats, stalls and wall bars to make up sequences depicting the story: for example, walk to market (a mat), climb a 'beanstalk' (wall bars), crawl underneath a bench to hide from the giant.

- Make up dances showing the ways different characters move: mother wrings her hands, the giant stamps around, Jack climbs and creeps, then chops down the beanstalk.

Outdoor opportunities

Have relay races using 'objects' stolen from the giant.

Play chasing games: the giant sits in the middle, and a child steals one of his belongings. He jumps up and chases the child around the outside of the circle back to their seat.

Resource sheet 1

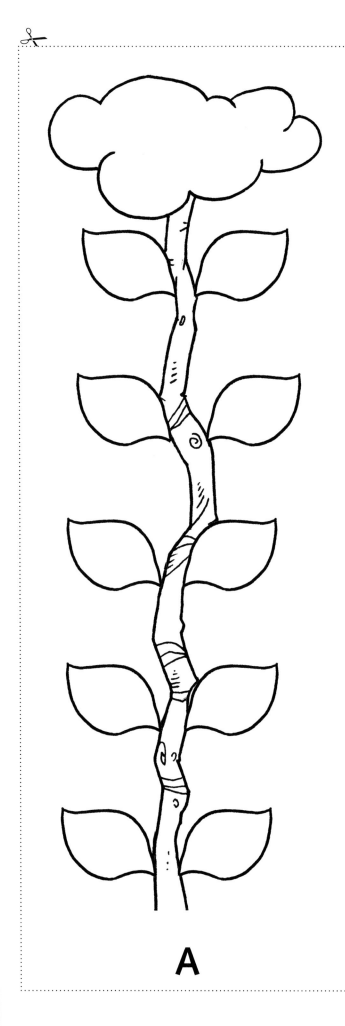

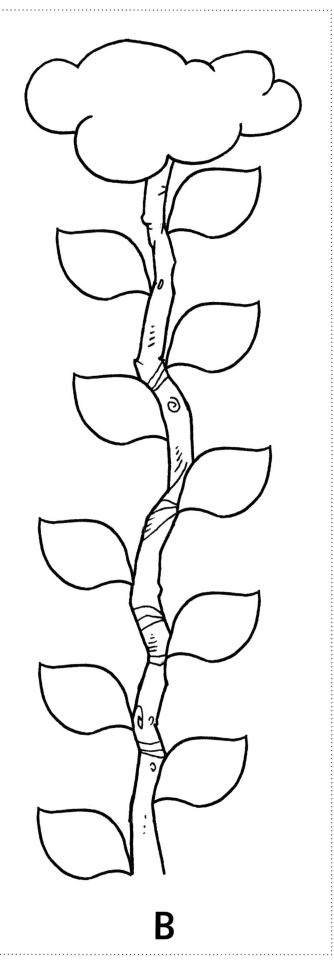

A

B

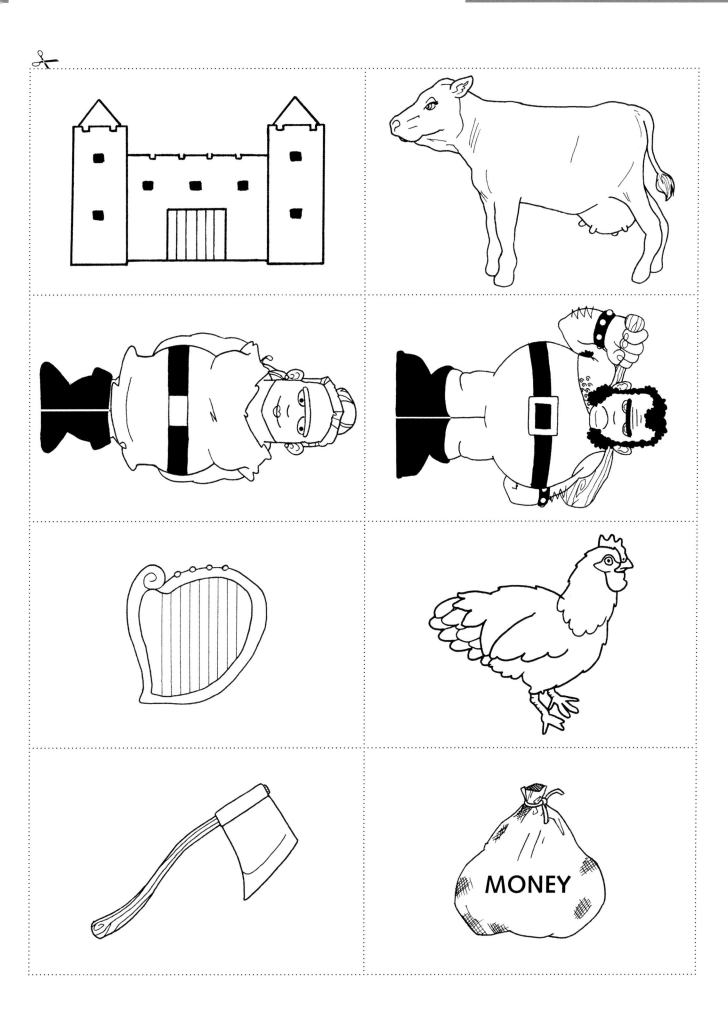

Dogger

This storybook by Shirley Hughes features Dave, who loses his much-loved toy dog Dogger. He searches the house for it, but fails to find it and is convinced he will not see his favourite toy again. But on a trip to the school fair, Dave sees Dogger among the toys for sale on a stall. He gets the money to buy Dogger, but finds the dog has already been sold. All is not lost, though: Bella, his older sister, generously swaps the huge teddy she has won with the girl who bought Dogger. Finally, the toy returns to its rightful owner.

Introduce the story as part of work on toys or fairs and fairgrounds or use it as a stimulus when doing work on families.

Maths overview

Using and applying mathematics

- Dave buys a toy car which costs 45p. He pays for it exactly. Which coins might he use? How many different ways could he pay? What if he only used silver coins?

- Have a selection of toys (use resource sheet 1 or real toys) and price them from 5p to 20p. Make up problems for children to solve: "Dave has 20p. What two toys might he buy?"; "Could he buy three toys?"; "He bought two toys and got 4p change. Which toys did he buy?" Children then make up their own problems for a partner to solve (they need to make sure they know the correct answer before handing over the problem).

- Lay out pictures of hoopla posts (use resource sheet 1). Each post is worth 5 points. Suppose you get your quoits onto two of the hooplas, what is your score? Suppose you manage to ring five of them? (Use counters to represent quoits.)

Counting and understanding number

- Set up a raffle. Number each prize with a different two- or three-digit number and record the numbers used on a communal sheet of paper, in any order. Children take turns to call out winning numbers from this sheet.

- Children pick a raffle ticket from a box and spin a spinner showing criteria such as 'odd', 'even', 'a multiple of 10', 'more than 30' … They win a counter if their number fits the criterion shown.

- Use masking tape or chalk to form a grid on the floor with 16 squares. Put a number card in each square, using a range of two-digit numbers. Children stand on a spot, throw five beanbags onto the grid and win the number cards from the squares where the beanbags land. They order the numbers that they have won and record these on a score card.

- Have a 'Guess how many in the jar' stall. Fill different-sized jars with buttons, conkers, cotton reels, small-world objects … Children estimate how many items are in each jar. At the end, children count the contents of each jar by grouping them in tens, fives or twos.

Handling data

- Sort a collection of real toys to make it easier for people visiting the stall. Discuss how to arrange the toys: by price, by type of toy?

- You need a collection of real toys. In secret, choose one to be your favourite and give children clues to help them identify which it is: "It has big ears, a black nose and no tail." Children then take on your role, playing with other children.

- Sort toys onto a Carroll diagram with criteria such as 'soft'/'not soft', 'ears'/'no ears'.

Knowing and using number facts

- Set up a coconut shy with 20 coconuts (use cards cut from resource sheet 1). Label the coconuts from 1 to 20. Bella has two balls: which coconuts could she knock down to score exactly 15? To score 18? Or 21?

- Use masking tape to make a grid on the floor with 16 squares. Write either 'double' or 'halve' in each square. Children choose a number card (only even numbers), then throw a beanbag. Depending on where it lands they either double or halve the number on their card.

Measuring

- Use a geared clock to show the times of various events in the story: for example, going home from school, looking for Dogger at night, going to bed. Show some 'silly' times and discuss why Dogger didn't go to school at 11 o'clock, and why tea time wouldn't be at 9 o'clock.

- Make a timetable for the fair: for example, the fair opens at 9 am, the fancy-dress competition starts at 12 o'clock. Pose problems such as: "Bella and Dave arrived at the fair at 10 o'clock. How long did they wait until the fancy-dress competition started?"

Dogger

Calculating

 Snapshot activities
See pages 50-51

 Close-up activity
See pages 52-53

Understanding shape

- Set up a lucky-dip stall. Wrap a selection of flat and solid shapes. Children pick a wrapped shape, feel and describe it and guess what shape it is before unwrapping it.

- You need a sheet of squared paper (with large squares) and some pictures of stalls (or use word cards). Label the squared paper with grid references: for example, A to F and 1 to 6. One child decides where to place a stall, using grid references, and tells their partner who places it there.

Calculating

Making arrays

• Represent repeated addition and arrays as multiplication

What you need: 1–30 number cards, counters

Explain a new fairground game. Children pick a number card, say the number and take that many counters (stick to numbers below 30). The challenge is to arrange the counters in lines to make an array: a single line does not count. If they can make an array, they write the corresponding multiplication and win a prize.

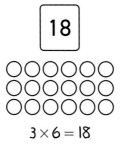

$3 \times 6 = 18$

Fancy-dress parade

• Use practical and informal written methods and related vocabulary to support multiplication and division, including calculations with remainders

What you need: Bag of 1p coins; bag of 10p coins

There is a bag of 1p coins for the winner of the fancy-dress parade. This year, there are three children in first place. Give the children a bag of 1p coins (a multiple of 3) to share between the three winners and ask them to record a division calculation to show their sharing.

Move on to a bag holding a number of coins that is not a multiple of 3.

Making it easier

Support children in making arrays with 10, 12 or 16 counters. Use square counters or cubes if available.

Making it harder

Give children 24 or 36 counters and ask them to find all the different arrays they can make with these. Discuss the fact that 4 rows of 6 is essentially the same as 6 rows of 4.

Making it easier

Support children in sharing out the coins systematically. Talk about how they can record this informally: for example, by drawing the sets of coins.

Making it harder

The bag contains 10p coins. What is the division calculation children should write?

Children explore which numbers of penny coins will share fairly between three prize winners, and which won't.

Skittles

• Subtract a multiple of 10 from any two-digit number mentally

What you need: Cards numbered from 70 to 100, 6 skittles, ball; cards numbered from 100 to 150

Children pick a card to find their starting number. They set up six skittles in a triangle formation. Each skittle represents 10. They roll a ball, aiming to knock down the skittles. Each skittle knocked over allows them to subtract 10 from their score. How many rolls does it take to get to a number below 10?

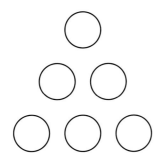

Making it easier

Children start with a number between 10 and 30. Each skittle is worth 1.

Making it harder

Children start with a number between 100 and 150. Label some skittles with 1 and some with 10. Children start with their given number and subtract the numbers on the skittles they knock over.

Code breaking

• Use the symbols +, −, ×, ÷ and = to record and interpret number sentences involving all four operations

What you need: –

Allocate numbers to each letter in the alphabet. Write a coded message meaning 'Find Dogger': for example, use $12 \div 2$, 3×3, $8 + 6$, $17 - 13$ for 'find'. Work with the class to decode the message.

Children then write their own coded message. They write the message in words and letters, rewrite it as numbers and make up a calculation for each number. Collect in completed messages and display them for other children to solve.

Making it easier

Children write a single word. Support them in the process of coding this word. Suggest they stick to addition and subtraction.

Making it harder

Expect children to work largely independently. Suggest they use multiplication and division.

A=1	B=2	C=3	D=4	E=5	F=6	G=7
H=8	I=9	J=10	K=11	L=12	M=13	N=14
O=15	P=16	Q=17	R=18	S=19	T=20	U=21
V=22	W=23	X=24	Y=25	Z=26		

Calculating

Ball in a bucket

- Add or subtract mentally a one-digit number or a multiple of 10 to or from any two-digit number
- Use practical and informal written methods to add and subtract two-digit numbers
- Use the symbols + and = to record and interpret number sentences

Setting up the activity (whole class or small group)

Set up a bucket stall with the children, labelling each bucket with a one- or two-digit number. Demonstrate how to play the game: you toss two balls into any buckets, score the number on each bucket and work out the total. Use resource sheet 2 to record your name, the numbers you scored and the total.

What number shall we choose to write on this bucket? How do you write that number?

Can you help me record my score? Which sign should I use?

What is a quick way to add my two numbers?

Development (teacher-led groups)

Children take turns at the bucket stall and record their score on resource sheet 2. Children have at least three turns each. Ask the group to use the table to find out which turn achieved the highest score.

Discuss with the children what equipment they can use to help them with their calculations, or whether they prefer to use informal jottings.

Will you need anything from the classroom to help you add those numbers?

How can you use a number line to add 5 and 7?

Show me how you worked out the answer.

Which is the highest score? And the next highest?

What you need

- Small buckets or tubs
- Sticky notes
- Ping-pong balls
- Resource sheet 2
- Wipeboards
- Number lines and 100-grids

Useful vocabulary

calculate, mental calculation, number sentence, sign, operation, symbol, add, plus, equals, problem, solve, method, table, record

Winding it down (whole class or small group)

Compare the tables submitted by the different groups and find the highest score overall (emphasise the score rather than the scorer and remind children about the significance of luck in this game).

Set one final challenge to work out as a group: someone scored 13; what buckets did they toss the balls into?

Did anyone here score that total or close to that total?

Can you explain what you did to find the answer to that problem?

Can the children

- record their calculation correctly?
- use number lines to support their calculations?
- use informal jottings to support their calculations?
- talk about the methods they used to solve the problems, and what they could try next time to make calculations easier?

Making it easier

Label the buckets with numbers to 10 or 20. Talk with the children about the best order to add their two numbers (starting with the larger number). Provide children with individual sheets to record their number sentence, and space for informal jottings.

Making it harder

Children investigate the highest/lowest score possible in one turn.

Extend to using three balls and adding three numbers.

Children find the overall total of each player in the game. Is the same person still the winner?

Links to other stories

Jack and the Beanstalk
Use 'magic' beans and plastic plant pots. (Stick the pots to the table or floor with double-sided tape.)

Growing Good
Use large seeds such as beans and partitioned seed trays.

Areas of learning

Understanding English, communication and languages

- Have the children ever lost anything special to them? Discuss how they lost it, how they felt, and whether they found it or not. Children then write about their loss.

- Write and design a 'Lost' poster for Dave to stick up in his street.

- Discuss the feelings in the story and complete a feelings graph. The vertical axis shows how happy Dave feels (sad at the bottom, happy at the top) and the horizontal axis is a time line. Draw a line for the graph to show how his feelings changed throughout the story.

- A child hides a soft toy in the classroom and gives the other children clues or directions to enable them to find it.

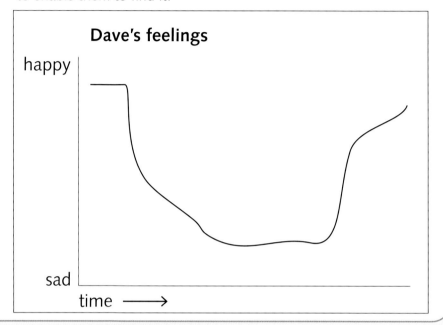

Dave's feelings

happy

sad

time ⟶

Scientific and technological understanding

- Make an electronic fairground game. Bend wire into a weird shape and stick the ends into a base; join one end to a buzzer using wires and crocodile clips. Direct an object (a conductor which is also attached to the buzzer) around the wire: if it touches the bent wire, the buzzer sounds and the game is lost.

- Make a fairground game. Children use magnetic tape to make magnetic rods and fish. They write numbers on the fish and see how high a score they can reach by catching fish with their rods.

- Use the computer to make posters with pictures and text for a school fair.

- Plan and carry out a class fair in groups. Use a video camera to record what children's stalls look like.

- Use columns in a word-processing program to write a newspaper report about the events at the fair. Insert clip-art pictures to add interest.

SUMMER FAIR

August 20th from 10am

Human, social and environmental understanding

- Compare Dave's local area and school to the children's local environment. What are the similarities and differences?

- Look closely at the pictures in the book. What are the clues that the book was written over 30 years ago? How have fashions changed in that time? How have they stayed the same?

- Discuss pictures of objects that children from different times in history, including the present, would consider special: a computer, hoop and stick, rag doll …

Understanding the arts and design

- Design a 'thank you' card for Dave to give Bella.

- Use fabric scraps to make bunting for a fairground stall.

- Children bring in a favourite teddy (or a photo of it). Use a range of media to make images of the teddies: clay, papier-mâché, felt …

- Children design a cart for a soft toy to travel on. Use wheels and axles with a simple frame to make the cart and discuss how to strengthen it.

Children test their cart to see how well it performs.

- Children design and make a hand puppet for a toy stall. Join two pieces of fabric together by sewing, using simple stitches, and decorate it with felt, ribbons and buttons.

- Learn the song 'Oh where, oh where has my little dog gone?'. Children keep time using percussion instruments.

Understanding physical health and well-being

- Pretend to be a toy: a jointed doll, a dog on wheels, a robot, a car. Make up a dance based on the way the toy moves.

Outdoor opportunities

Set up tables and games outside and have a class fair. Bring in second-hand books and toys to sell for a penny each. Have activities such as hoopla (targets for children to throw small hoops or quoits over) and a coconut shy (objects on a bench for children to throw soft balls at).

Resource sheet 1

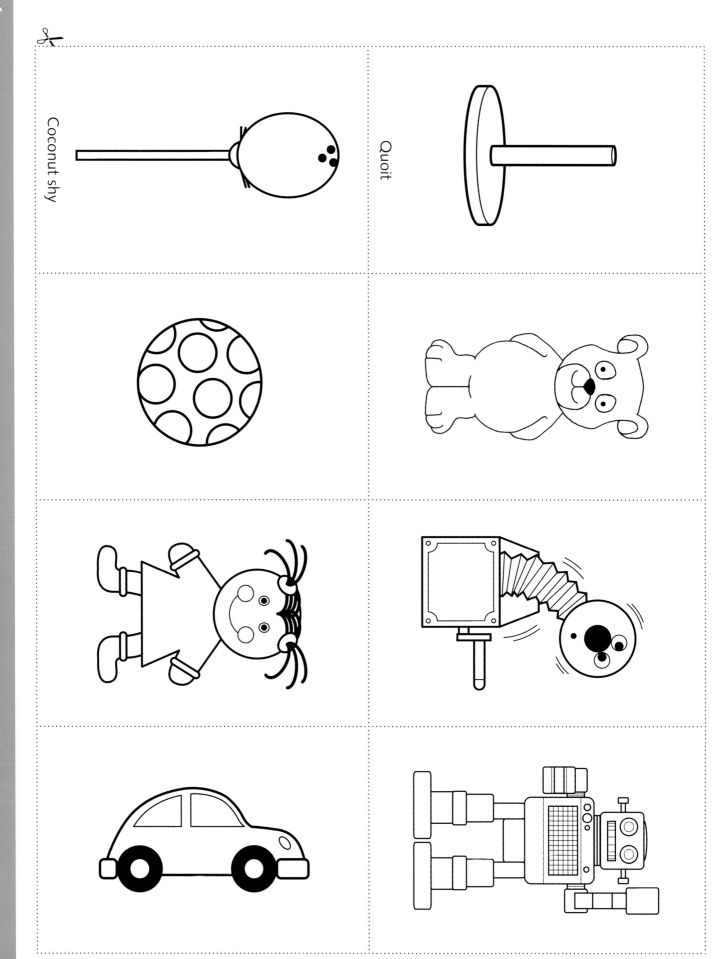

Coconut shy

Quoit

Resource sheet 2

Name	My number sentence	Total score

Snow White

Snow White and the Seven Dwarfs was a well-known tale all over the world even before the Brothers Grimm first collected it in the late 19th century. It is the story of a young princess, Snow White, whose jealous and wicked stepmother tries to kill her. Luckily, Snow White meets seven dwarfs who become her friends. The wicked queen finds out where Snow White is staying and eventually manages to poison her, sending her into a coma. Thankfully, a king's son arrives to wake her with a magical kiss!

Use the story for its own merits or as part of work on fairy tales, good and bad behaviour or homes.

Maths overview

Using and applying mathematics

- How many slices of bread does Snow White need to make a sandwich for each dwarf, to take to work? What if they want two sandwiches each?

- How can Snow White divide a cuboid-shaped cake fairly between herself and her seven friends?

- Design a repeating pattern of shapes to frame the magic mirror. If somebody disrupts the pattern, can children spot the mistake and repair it?

Counting and understanding number

- When the huntsman took Snow White into the forest, they gathered leaves, fir cones, pebbles ... Show children the gathered items, ask them to estimate how many there are of each item and to check by counting.

- Snow White helps the dwarfs record the amount of gold they have mined each day, to send a report to the mine owner. Take the role of a

dwarf and read out a series of two- and three-digit numbers. Children record these in figures or in words.

- Each day, the dwarfs record how many gold nuggets they have mined to the nearest 10. Provide a table with the day and number of nuggets found. Children use a

number line to work out the nearest 10 and record this in a third column.

Day	Number of nuggets	Rounds to
Monday	34	30
Tuesday	46	
Wednesday	42	

Knowing and using number facts

- Write multiples of 10 on cards showing a bag of gold (use resource sheet 1); this shows how many gold nuggets a bag contains. Children help the dwarfs put their bags in pairs with a total of 100 nuggets.

- Repeat this activity with cards showing numbers to 19. Children put them in pairs to make 20.

- Make apple dominoes. Draw an apple outline (use resource sheet 1) with a line down the middle. Write the same number on each side of the line (or draw apple pips) and record the total on the back. Hang up the apples. If a child can see the number on the reverse, what are the numbers on the front?

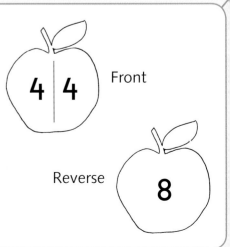

Calculating

- The dwarfs are cold at night. Snow White is going to knit them some blankets. If each dwarf needs two blankets, how many must she knit? Children make up other number problems about the dwarfs' home.

- Snow White is sharing out carrot sticks between the dwarfs' plates for dinner. She has 30 (or 20 or 35) sticks. How many do they get each and how many are left over?

- Provide apple- or mirror-shaped cards, each showing a different number or symbol (0, 1, 2, ... , −, +, ×, ÷, =). Children use the cards to make a number sentence. They then turn one card face down and challenge a friend to work out what it shows.

Measuring

- Children scoop up a spoon- or cupful of yellow cubes to represent gold and find out how much it weighs.

- Provide wide strips of paper of various lengths. Children estimate which strip will be a suitable length from which to make themselves a crown and see how well it fits round their head.

- The dwarfs are 1 m tall. Children measure strips of paper with metre rules in order to make the outline of a bed to fit a dwarf.

- The dwarfs are 1 m tall. Would the children be able to walk through a dwarf door without bending down?

Snow White

Understanding shape

 Snapshot activities
See pages 62-63

 Close-up activity
See pages 64-65

Handling data

- Help the children carry out a survey to decide the most popular choice of fruit to use in tempting Snow White. Record and present the findings, using ICT.

- Children complete a picture of the wicked stepmother, using the outline on resource sheet 2. Sort the completed pictures on a Venn, Carroll or tree diagram and discuss what the sets have in common.

Understanding shape

Buildings

- Visualise common 2D shapes and 3D solids
- Identify shapes from pictures of them in different positions and orientations

What you need:
Twenty 3D solids, camera; 2D shapes

Children build a simple cottage or palace, using twenty 3D solids. Take photographs of the building from two or three different angles. Demolish the building and challenge children to rebuild it from the photographs.

Making it easier

Make a flat picture using 2D shapes

Making it harder

Children work in pairs with identical sets of shapes and a barrier between them. One child makes a cottage, describing at the same time how to build it to a friend who makes an identical one the other side of the barrier.

Saving Snow White

- Follow and give instructions involving position, direction and movement
- Recognise and use whole, half and quarter turns, both clockwise and anticlockwise

What you need: 25 tiles, small-world objects

Lay out 25 tiles on the floor in a 5 by 5 array and put hazards on some of the tiles (slimy toad, pond, snake …): this is the forest through which the prince is riding. But it is a foggy day, and the prince is struggling to reach Snow White without meeting any of the hazards. One child acts as Snow White, lying on the floor the other side of the array from the prince. Children guide the prince to Snow White, using the language of direction and turning.

Making it easier

Help children use simple language such as 'forward', 'backward', 'left' and 'right'.

Making it harder

Provide a drawing of the 5 by 5 array and ask children to write a set of instructions to guide the prince through the forest.

Making a cottage

• Visualise common 2D shapes and 3D solids

• Make and describe shapes, referring to their properties

What you need: A cube and a square-based pyramid

Children make a simple cottage shape using only
two 3D solids: a cube and a square-based pyramid.

They work out how to make a net of the shape using
ready-made shapes that easily slot into each other or squares
and triangles cut from card. They test the net by folding it up
to recreate a cottage, which they then decorate.

Making it easier

Help children analyse the shape
and count how many squares
and triangles they will need.

Making it harder

Challenge children to make a
net for a larger cottage shape
and describe what it will look
like when folded up.

Magic mirror

• Identify reflective symmetry in patterns and 2D shapes and
  draw lines of symmetry in shapes

What you need: Resource sheet 2, flat or sticky shapes

Children decorate the frame of the magic mirror on resource
sheet 2, using flat shapes or sticky shapes. The frame should
be symmetrical. They draw a symmetrical face in the reflective
part of the mirror.

Making it easier

Provide just a few different
kinds of shape in a limited
palette of colours.

Making it harder

One child draws half a face
in the 'mirror', and their
friend completes it, making
it symmetrical.

Understanding shape

Making blankets

- Visualise common 2D shapes and 3D solids
- Make and describe shapes, referring to their properties
- Recognise and use whole, half and quarter turns, both clockwise and anticlockwise

Setting up the activity (whole class or small group)

The dwarfs' beds look a real mess as all their blankets have holes, but the dwarfs refuse to have new blankets. Snow White says that she will make them some bedcovers to hide the old blankets. She wants to put interesting patterns on the bedcovers, but only wants to use one shape for each dwarf so that she knows whose bedcover is whose.

Talk about the children's own bedding. Does it have patterns or pictures on it?

Show children a range of sponge shapes; identify which ones show geometric shapes and which ones represent real objects. Children choose a sponge and explore how to make its shape look different by turning.

Tell me about the patterns on your duvet/blankets/curtains at home.

How can you make this shape look different?

Can you find a shape that looks the same when it is turned through a quarter or a half turn?

Development (teacher-led groups)

Each child has a piece of scrap paper on which to test out shapes until they find one they think the dwarfs will like. Allow them time to explore turning, and printing with, different shapes before they commit to the shape they will be using. Once they have chosen their shape, ask them to tell you something about their shape and explain why they have chosen it.

Give each child a large piece of paper or fabric and ask them to print the first row of their pattern, remembering to turn the sponge each time: quarter turn, half turn, quarter turn, half turn – or whatever pattern they chose. When they get to the end of the line, they decide whether to use another colour for the next line, and whether to alter their pattern (but stick to the same shape).

Can you describe the pattern you are going to make?

What will you do at the end of the line? What could you try next?

What you need

- A range of shapes cut from sponge to print with (include geometric shapes and 'real' shapes such as animals or flowers)
- Scrap paper for experimenting
- Large piece of material or paper to print onto
- Paints (fabric paints if printing onto material)

Useful vocabulary

flat, curved, square, rectangle, rectangular, triangle, triangular, circle, circular, pentagon, hexagon, octagon, pattern, direction, clockwise, anticlockwise, quarter turn, straight line

What do you notice about Lily's pattern?

Do any of your prints look the same/different?

Winding it down (whole class or small group)

Gather the children together and look at the bedspreads they have made. Can anyone describe someone else's pattern and how they made it?

Next, answer the phone to one of the dwarfs who is asking how the bedspreads are coming on. Ask a child to stand up and display their blanket and describe to the dwarf on the phone how they made the pattern.

At a later date, children can paint a dwarf to cut out and stick underneath their bedspread. These would make a great display.

Can you tell me about your pattern? Describe it to a friend!

Look at these two blankets. Can you see any things that are the same/different about them?

Can the children

- describe shapes, using appropriate mathematical language?

- explain and justify their choice of shape?

- demonstrate an understanding of turning when printing?

- describe and talk about their pattern?

- explain how they approach and tackle the problem?

- take time to investigate and carefully consider their choice or do they rush?

Making it easier

Make simple repeating patterns without turning. Ask the children to talk about these. Can they look at a friend's pattern and predict what will come next?

Making it harder

Children record the instructions for making their pattern so that Snow White can lend their instructions to her friends who can then make identical bedspreads.

Links to other stories

Jack and the Beanstalk
Children print patterns using real leaves or leaf-shaped sponges.

Areas of learning

Understanding English, communication and languages

- Write alternative rhymes for the magic mirror: "Mirror, mirror on the wall, who is the meanest/cleverest/kindest of them all?" In a 'mirror frame', draw characters from well-known stories who display that trait.

- Write instructions for Snow White, telling her how to carry out a household chore such as sweeping the floors or making the beds. Use sequencing language and time adverbials.

Scientific and technological understanding

- The dwarfs' job is to dig for gold. Give children trays of different substances such as sand or grit mixed with 'gold' (small yellow or gold beads) and ask them to think of ways to separate the gold from the other material. Measure how much gold they have managed to collect.

- The queen wants to tempt Snow White with a poisonous flower. Which type of flower could she use? Provide children with some information books on flowers and ask them to select some she might use.

- Use a paint program to make a portrait of the beautiful but wicked stepmother.

Human, social and environmental understanding

- Children look in mirrors and draw self-portraits. They then draw how they might look when they are older. Discuss how the children expect to change physically.

- Look at household tools that Snow White might have used (washtub and washboard, spinning wheel, broom). Compare them to what people use nowadays (washing machine, ready-made clothes, vacuum cleaner).

- Look at pictures of palaces and cottages from around the world.

- Discuss the feelings of jealousy and envy. Talk about how the witch could have dealt with these feelings more positively. Relate this to times in the children's lives when they have felt jealous.

- The dwarfs helped Snow White by offering her a place to stay. When have the children helped someone and what did they do?

Understanding the arts and design

- Show children the outline of a magic mirror, with the 'glass' revealing a photo of part of something in the children's local environment (the corner of the school building or part of a playground swing). Children look at the image, discuss what it might be and complete the picture with a drawing.

- Make puppets of the main characters and use these to perform a puppet show.

- Listen to pieces of classical music to illustrate parts of the story; for example, *Flight of the Bumble Bee* by Nikolai Rimsky-Korsakov when the dwarfs work in the mine or *Mars the Bringer of War* by Gustav Holst to depict the wicked queen. Children talk about how the music makes them feel, then draw a picture or pattern to illustrate this.

- Children work together to make a piece of music to show Snow White's feelings when she is lost in the woods and feeling scared.

Outdoor opportunities

Make rubbings of different wall surfaces. Back in class, decide which are suitable for the stepmother's palace and which for the cottage.

Understanding physical health and well-being

- Children work in pairs. One is Snow White or the prince she marries, and the other is their reflection in a mirror. Children decide on a sequence of movements, learn them and show them to the class.

- Make up dances depicting Snow White's chores.

Outdoor opportunities

Play at being the huntsman. Instead of a bow and arrows to hit a picture of a boar, try using beanbags.

Resource sheet 1

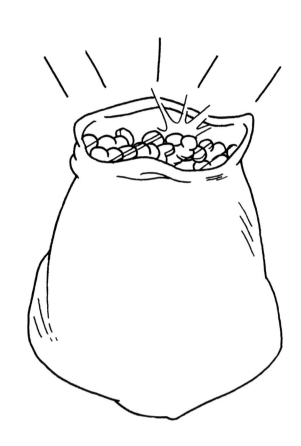

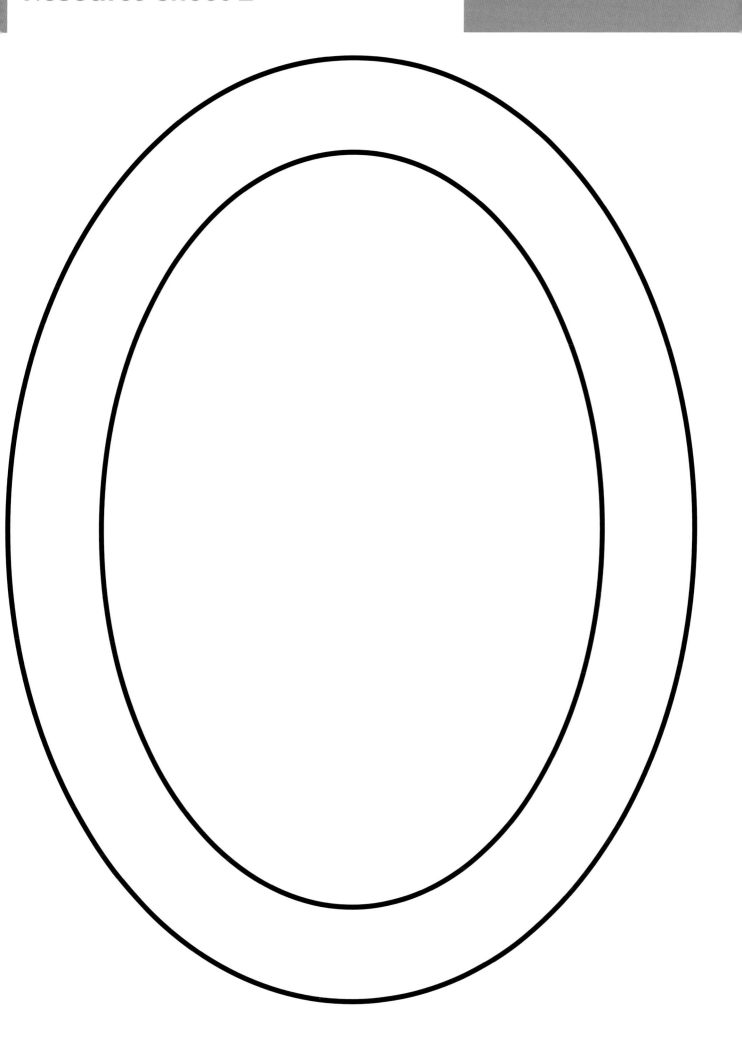

The Jolly Postman

Janet and Allan Ahlberg's wonderful and imaginative storybook about a friendly and busy postman who cycles around Fairy-tale Land, delivering all types of exciting mail to the familiar characters who live there.

The book is full of 'real' letters, in envelopes: enough to delight and engage any child. Use the book and its contents in topics on journeys, post offices, letters and cards, jobs or celebrations.

Maths overview

Using and applying mathematics

- The cost of a stamp depends on the longest dimension of an envelope (which may be the width or the height). Make a poster showing whatever criteria you choose. Provide envelopes of different sizes and ask the children to draw stamps on them, totalling the correct postage.

Size of envelope	Costs
less than 15 cm	15p
between 15 cm and 30 cm	30p
more than 30 cm	45p

- The Jolly Postman has a parcel which costs 55p to post. The sender has put on seven stamps. Each stamp was either 10p or 5p. Which stamps were on the parcel?

- The stamps for a parcel cost the same amount of pennies as the grams they weigh. Children draw the correct value of stamps on some parcels.

Counting and understanding number

- The postman has a busy day ahead of him, with a pile of postcards to deliver (use up to 100 old postcards and greetings cards). Explore ways to count them by grouping them in twos, fives and tens.

- Give each child a number card to represent their house number. Children organise themselves in order and tell you which house numbers are missing.

- Cinderella and the prince were asking for 10 (or 8 or 16) million pounds for their palace. It didn't sell, so they halved the price. What was the new price?

- Mrs Bear has a square birthday cake. How many different ways can she cut it into quarters?

Handling data

- Find some unusual containers (washing-up bottle, yogurt pot, matchbox) and put small toys in them as presents. Seal them up and send them to the sorting office. There, they get sorted in various ways: 'curved sides', 'cube shape', 'has a circular face' … Children decide how to sort the parcels and check each one to see if it fits the description. Move on to sorting by two criteria onto Venn and Carroll diagrams. Finally, children open the parcels, just for fun.

- Use the parcels from the previous activity and add some stamps to them. Give criteria such as 'Today, the Jolly Postman is only delivering parcels with flat faces/curved faces/stamps worth more than 50p'. Which ones will he/won't he be delivering?

- Sort the stamped parcels from the two previous activities onto a tree or Venn diagram yourself, then show it to the children. Tell the children that the labels on the tree diagram have come off. Can they work out what should be on them?

Knowing and using number facts

- New houses are being built in Two Street (where houses are numbered only with multiples of 2), but the houses do not have any numbers on. Children draw a street of houses and label each door with a number.

- The Giant is 100 today. He can't invite everybody to his party, so he is asking only people whose age is a multiple of 10. What ages might people in the story be and will any of them get invited?

- There are 15 people at Goldilocks' party. If everybody eats 2 biscuits, how many do they eat altogether? Only 13 of them like cupcakes. How many cupcakes does Goldilocks need so that they can have two each?

Calculating

- Explain that Goldilocks has 10 guests at her party and has to get party bags ready. Each person gets 5 (or 3 or 8) gifts in their bag. How many gifts does she have to buy altogether?

- The post office till has broken, and the cashier has to work out all the totals on paper. Give the children some simple word problems and ask them to record these: for example, Mrs Bear buys 3 stamps at 5 pence each. Which operations can they use to work out the answer? What is the answer? How can children record the calculation?

The Jolly Postman

Measuring

 Snapshot activities
See pages 74-75

 Close-up activity
See pages 76-77

Understanding shape

- Children use building blocks or construction equipment to make a fairy-tale house. But they cannot use whatever pieces they want: they must ask a friend to find the first few pieces for them, from a box in the middle of the table. Encourage them to give accurate descriptions such as:

"I need several of the long red brick shapes … And two of the flat green rectangles."

- Talk about right angles. Demonstrate how the corner of an envelope is a right angle. Children make some envelopes with and without right-angled corners.

Measuring

Time problems

- Use units of time (seconds, minutes, hours, days) and know the relationships between them
- Read the time to the quarter hour
- Identify time intervals, including those that cross the hour

What you need: Geared clocks

Ask the children simple word problems relating to time. They use geared clocks to show and work out the times. For example:

The Jolly Postman leaves his house on foot at 6.30 am and arrives at Three Bears Cottage at 7:15. How much time did his journey take?

The Jolly Postman leaves Three Bears Cottage at 7:30 am. It takes him 1 hour to walk to Gingerbread Bungalow. What time does he arrive there?

On a day when he uses his bike, each journey takes about 15 minutes. How long does it take him to complete his rounds? How long does it take him on a windy day when it takes double the time?

Weighing parcels

- Estimate and measure weight, choosing and using standard units and suitable measuring instruments

What you need: Wrapped parcel of various weights, weighing instruments; cubes

Provide children with some wrapped parcels of various weights and a range of weighing instruments. The three bears are sending presents to their friends. Show the children a list of prices showing how much it costs to post parcels. Children record the weight of each parcel and the cost of posting it.

Parcel postage	
up to 100 g	50p
100 g to 200 g	£1
200 g to 300 g	£1.50
300 g to 400 g	£1.90
400 g to 500 g	£2.30
over 500 g	£3

Making it easier

Focus on problems relating to whole and half hours.

Making it harder

Children make up word problems for their friends. Remind them that they need to know the answers themselves in order to check their friends' work.

Making it easier

Use units such as cubes to weigh the parcels. Support children as they work.

Making it harder

Children make a parcel to fit each category by filling boxes with objects.

Carrying parcels

• Estimate, compare and measure weight, choosing and using standard units and suitable measuring instruments

What you need: Wrapped parcels of various weights, weighing instruments; carrier bags

Provide children with some wrapped parcels of various weights and a range of weighing instruments. The Jolly Postman is only allowed to carry a maximum of 5 kg of parcels in his sack. The children fill a sack with the maximum number of parcels he can carry. What is the weight of the remaining parcels? How many trips will he need to make?

Making it easier

The postman is only allowed to carry parcels weighing 1 kg or less. Children sort the parcels into 'OK' and 'too heavy'.

Making it harder

The postman's sack has ripped, so he borrows some paper carrier bags. Help him balance the weight of the parcels fairly between the two bags to avoid straining them too much.

Weighing scale

• Read the numbered divisions on a scale and interpret the divisions between them

What you need: Kitchen scales, resource sheet 2, short sticks

As a preliminary, look at some kitchen scales (with a circular scale if possible) with the children.

The scale on the letter weighing machine at the post office has got ink spilt on it. The children are to help make a new one. Provide a circular scale to number in multiples of 10 g (from 0 g to 100 g; see the second scale on resource sheet 2).

Making it easier

Use the first scale on resource sheet 2 and label it in kilograms.

Making it harder

Use the shorter divisions, for multiples of 5 g, but leave them unnumbered. Point to one of these divisions and ask the children to say what its value is.

When they have finished, children take turns to hide one or more of the numbers and challenge a friend to say what weights are hidden.

Move on to using short sticks as weighing scale pointers. Announce a weight; children use their sticks to show the scale registering that weight.

Measuring

Postmarks

- Use units of time (minutes, hours, days) and know the relationships between them
- Read the time to the quarter hour

Setting up the activity (whole class or small group)

Ask the children if they know how to tell when a letter was sorted at the post office. Show them some real envelopes and point out the postmark.

Recreate a postmark from the book on the board and ask the children to identify what information it gives (time of day, date, place posted). Provide pairs of children with a set of 'envelopes' from resource sheet 1. Children agree with their partners when each letter was stamped and which one was stamped first.

They then put the four envelopes in order of posting, according to their postmarks.

What day was this letter posted? How do you know that?

Were all the letters posted on the same day?

How many letters were posted on June 12th?

Which letter was posted first? Do you look at the date or the time to find out?

Show me where it says the time of stamping.

Development (teacher-led groups)

Provide each child with an envelope and ask them to address it to a fairy-tale character of their choice. They draw a stamp on it and a postmark. Ask them to choose a time and date from the present month to put on their postmark. Give children plastic circles to draw around to get the shape of the postmark and provide real calendars from which children can choose a date.

Support children in recording the time, date and place of posting.

What information will you need to record on the postmark?

In some villages there are no collections on a Sunday. So if you post a letter on Sunday, when will it be stamped at the post office?

Can you use the calendar to find out which day of the week May 13th is?

Is there a 35th of May? How do you know that?

What you need

- Real envelopes with postmarks on
- Sets of envelopes with postmarks (see resource sheet 1)
- Blank envelopes
- Large plastic circles
- Calendars

Useful vocabulary

before, after, earlier, later, time, month, day, hour, minute, quarter to, quarter past, days of the week, months of the year

Winding it down (whole class or small group)

Bring the children back to the carpet with their envelopes and ask for ideas about how to put them in order of stamping. Work with the children to sort the letters according to date, then sort the letters for each date by time of day. Refer to a calendar as necessary to check the order of dates.

Talk about how a birthday card must be posted a day or two before someone's birthday if it is to arrive on time. Ask children for their own birthday dates; they tell a partner when cards must be posted to arrive on time for their birthday.

These two letters were stamped on the same day. How do we find out which was stamped earlier?

Which of these two letters was stamped first? How much time was there between when this letter and that letter were stamped?

How many letters were posted on November 20th?

Can the children

• say the months of the year in order?

• say the days of the week in order?

• show an understanding of the relationships between days, weeks and months?

• read and record times (whole hours, half hours, quarter hours) correctly?

• order envelopes by date of stamping?

Making it easier

Make postmarks all with the same date, with the time of stamping on the hour (9:00 am, 11:00 am, and so on), and order these.

Making it harder

Look at real postmarks, and those from the book, that involve writing dates as numerals, including Roman numerals, and help children interpret these.

20. V. 86   10.03.09

Links to other stories

Cinderella
The prince and his friends send out invitations to a ball. The children write envelopes for the invitations and put the letters in order of stamping.

Areas of learning

Understanding English, communication and languages

- Write letters and postcards to fairy-tale characters and address envelopes to put them in. Put them in a 'post box' so that the Jolly Postman can deliver them.

- Read the letter Goldilocks sends to Mr and Mrs Bear. Ask the children how they think Baby Bear feels about the letter. If they were Baby Bear, would they go to Goldilocks' party?

- Imagine you are going on a 'magic carpet tour' as Jack (of Beanstalk fame) does. Write a postcard from the trip to a fairy-tale character of your choice.

- Visit a post office, then set up a role-play area as a post office. Provide postage stamps, stamp pad and stamp, envelopes, writing paper, money …

- Look at the adverts the witch receives. Would they make the witch want to buy something? Design adverts to sell items to other fairy-tale characters.

- Write a 'For sale' advert for Cinderella's palace (or any of the homes in the book). Include descriptions of the rooms and gardens, using persuasive language.

Beautiful large palace. Big enough for a large family. You can hold good parties here. £1000

Scientific and technological understanding

- Look at a bicycle or tricycle and work out how the pedals make the wheels go round. How could the postman make his bike go faster or slower? How do the brakes work?

- Set a toy car (instead of a bicycle) off down a slope and explore how to make it stop without crashing it.

- Pretend the classroom door is a front door and the children are postal delivery people. What height would be best for the letterbox? What size and shape should it be? What are the pros and cons of having a really large letterbox?

- Design a container to attach to the letterbox on a front door, to catch letters that are put through the slot.

- Use recording equipment to make recordings of traditional stories for younger children.

- Videorecord children's own adverts for 'Hobgoblin Supplies Ltd'.

Human, social and environmental understanding

- Imagine that the Jolly Postman can travel back in time to deliver letters to people from the past. Ask the children to write letters to people from history topics they have studied: for example, Oliver Cromwell or Florence Nightingale.

- Talk about the 'traditional' stories and rhymes. Ask the children to find out which are their parents' and grandparents' favourite traditional stories.

- Look at the clothes the characters are wearing and discuss which are modern and which are old-fashioned.

How can the children tell the diffference?

Understanding the arts and design

- Make a collaborative class collage of the Jolly Postman's journey.

- Look at some real stamps. Design some celebratory stamps for a royal wedding, sporting event or other special occasion.

- Explain that the postman's bike got crushed when the giant stood on it. Can children design and make an alternative mode of transport? What materials will they use, and what advantages/diasadvantages do they foresee those materials will have?

Understanding physical health and well-being

- Talk about the importance of exercising to stay healthy. Was the postman fit? How far might he cycle in a day? Could the children cycle that far?

Outdoor opportunities

Use bicycles and other objects (space hoppers, stilts) to explore ways of travelling. Which use most effort? Which are fast and which are slow?

✂

Baby Bear
Three Bears Cottage
The Woods
HO2 NEY

NORTH POLE
12 JUNE
2009
11.10 am

80p

Jack's Mum
Beanstalk House
Giant Road
Beanshire
MU14MM

PIPERS LAND
13 MAY
2009
3.00 pm

55p

HRH Cinderella
New Palace
Princedom Lane
Royalshire
RO6 5AL

JILL'S HILL
12 JUNE
2009
4.15 pm

35p

The Jolly Postman
Sorting Office
Storyland
ST15 XYZ

THE MOON
11 JUNE
2009
9.00 am

35p

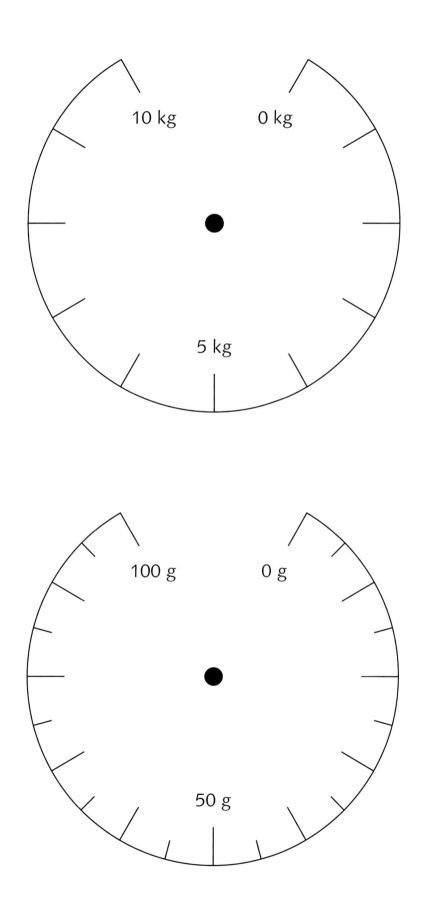

Growing Good

When the box factory is knocked down, leaving some unused ground, Samuel and Grandad Jess know exactly what they would like to do with it, and their work to create allotments begins. However, Steve Tott, their neighbour, is not happy with their plans and petitions for a car park to be built there.

Samuel and Grandad Jess not only need to persuade the locals but also the planners that gardens would be the best use of the space. A sense of community develops as planting starts, and the planners are persuaded. Samuel and Grandad Jess's dreams come true.

Growing Good by Bernard Ashley and Anne Wilson is a true celebration of community life and good growing. Introduce it when you are doing work on growing food or as part of a project on homes and communities.